FORGIVING

THE

PEOPLE

YOU

LOVE

TO

HATE

FORGIVING THE PEOPLE YOU LOVE TO HATE

Judy Logue

Liguori
ONE LIGUORI DRIVE
LIGUORI MO 63057-9999
314.464.2500

Imprimi Potest:
Richard Thibodeau, C.SS.R.
Provincial, Denver Province
The Redemptorists

Imprimatur:
+ Paul A. Zipfel, V.G.
Auxiliary Bishop, Archdiocese of St. Louis

ISBN 0-7648-0063-9
Library of Congress Catalog Card Number: 96-78939

Scripture quotations are from the *New American Bible*, copyright ©
1991, 1986, and 1970 by the Confraternity of Christian Doctrine, 3211
Fourth Street N.E., Washington, DC 20017-1194, and are used by
permission. All rights reserved.

Cover design by Wendy Barnes

DEDICATION

For my parents
Lois Boudreaux O'Brien
and
Floyd Percy O'Brien
with ever deepening gratitude,
and for the men and women who,
in workshops and over coffee,
shared with me
their stories of alienation and reconciliation

CONTENTS

ACKNOWLEDGMENTS

I t is a pleasure to thank the many people whose encouragement and suggestions made this book possible. The late Father Louis Miller, CSSR, and Father Pat Kaler, CSSR, who first encouraged me to write and brought me to Liguori Publications; Kass Dotterweich, my editor, who picked up where Louie and Pat left off; Father Vic Karls, CSSR, who gave me the opportunity to facilitate retreats; and the people who worked and retreated at Villa Redeemer Retreat Center in Glenview, Illinois. You started me on this journey.

My gratitude goes to the good folks who introduced me to the power of personal stories and the discovery of our God within them: the participants in the Rite of Christian Initiation for Adults at St. Francis Xavier Parish, Wilmette, Illinois for the past twelve years; the men and women who worked with me at the forgiveness workshops from Louisiana to Ireland; the women who accepted the invitation to our Martha Retreats; and the early writings of John Powell, SJ, who first showed me how psychology and theology fit together. Thank you all for your stories.

My study and writing has been greatly enriched and facilitated by my friends, professors, and colleagues at Catholic Theological Union in Chicago, especially Steve Bevans, SVD, Dianne Bergant, OSA, Gary Riebe-Estrella, SVD, and John Linnan, CSV; those at the Institute of Pastoral Studies at Loyola University, especially Drs. Joan Scanlon, OP and James Zullo, CFC so many years ago; and by my good friends Linda Leahy and Jeanie Egmon, who read chapters and offered helpful critiques. Thank you all for encouraging me and for pushing me.

I am especially indebted to those who read the manuscript and graciously offered invaluable suggestions: Dr. Patricia O'Connell Killen of Pacific Lutheran University in Tacoma; Loretta Brady, MSW; Drs. Jim and Evelyn Whitehead; and Robert Schreiter, CPPS, Catholic Theological Union. I deeply appreciate your time and your expertise. You went above and beyond the call of friendship.

Finally to my family: Ed, my companion on the journey, and to Scott, Rosemary, Michael O'Brien, Laura, John Patrick, and Virginia, and to Ellie, Maggie, and Noah: Thank you for your love and support. I am proud to be part of your stories.

THE INVITATION

Do you ever find yourself remembering and reliving negative feelings and events of long ago? Do you ever regret "turning the other cheek" just to keep peace in the family, despite your feelings of pain or anger? Do you sometimes wonder if genuine forgiveness is really possible? If this describes you, read on. This invitation is for you.

PRESENCE

Your presence is requested. You are invited to take a journey that begins in a place called alienation and travels toward a destination called reconciliation. You will travel many different terrains, parts of which will be rough and bumpy. If you pay close attention, however, much of your journey will be surprising and insightful.

Participation

Your participation is requested. You will be asked to engage in writing exercises that are intended to help you along the journey. These exercises have been tested in the laboratory of human experience for many years. Hundreds of retreat and workshop participants have helped develop and refine them.

Your writing will help you think more clearly. It will slow you down and allow your thoughts, feelings, and memories to come quietly to the surface of your consciousness. I recommend you use a journal for your writing exercises.

The sections titled *For further reflection* are for your personal thoughts. You may want to share these thoughts with a trusted friend or friends. Sharing your stories moves you to hear yourself in a different way. Friends offer much needed support, comfort, and challenge.

Courage

Your courage is requested. Forgiveness is a scary thing. All of us hold resentments that are very familiar and comfortable. There are people we love to hate; we cannot imagine life without them. A decision to participate in the possibility of change takes courage, but you can do it.

My own journey

I cannot mark the exact moment when I set out on my own journey through forgiveness. It must have been about twenty years ago. I clearly remember that when I heard someone say, "Forgiveness is a decision," the idea exploded in my brain. A whole new world of possibilities opened to me. There was much I needed to forgive in my life, but I had always thought that forgiveness was more of a feeling that came over me rather than an action I could initiate. I was fascinated and hopeful, and I began to entertain questions.

My exploration was not a careful, focused study, however; it was more like looking at something out of the corner of my eye. I teased out questions like: "Is forgiveness more than pious platitudes?" "Can forgiveness be taken out of the pulpit and the pages of romance novels and brought into the lives of everyday folks?" "Is there a psychology to forgiveness?" "Is there a way to map the process of forgiveness?" "Is forgiveness really possible in all situations?"

I know these were the right questions because answers began to present themselves. Certain articles and books about forgiveness were helpful in theory, although none helped me forgive anyone in particular. Then there were the generous participants who attended the forgiveness workshops, people who shared their stories and struggles. In their willing hearts, and in my efforts to come to terms with alienation and resentment in my own relationships, I discovered most of what is in this book. Gradually a process of "how to forgive" began to emerge. I shared my ideas and feelings with friends, and they in turn critiqued and encouraged me. Finally I mustered up courage and began to write about the thorny subject and practice of forgiveness.

The provisions for my journey of forgiveness continue to be presence, courage, participation through writing, and the willing ears and hearts of my close friends. I am asking these same things of you, for I know they will serve you well. The journey is worth the effort it takes to read this book and work with the exercises. When you finish, you will be able to glimpse a new sense of freedom on the horizon.

PART I

ALIENATION

1

FORGIVE AND FORGET?

Ve know a great deal about forgiveness. We have learned from our personal experiences of loving and relating with others.

We have also learned about forgiveness from the messages expressed by the world around us. Who can forget those often-quoted words from the conclusion of *Love Story* by Eric Segal: "Love is never having to say you're sorry." Romantic message that it is, however, it simply does not ring true in the experience of everyday, ordinary relationships. Yet, surprisingly, it remains a compelling message.

FORGIVENESS IS NOT...

Those who took *Love Story* to heart internalized the message that relationships should be just like that: never having to say "I'm sorry." In the process, these people learned to bypass forgiveness. This message is only one of many that have taught us what to do when we feel hurt.

When I ask workshop participants what they know about forgiveness, "forgive and forget" is one of the first phrases offered. Many believe that this is a biblical command, but it isn't. This familiar phrase was coined in the fourteenth century when poets of the late Middle Ages sang of the joys of romantic love. But we all know from personal experience that forgiveness is simply not that easy.

The messages about forgiveness come at us from many angles. The Hebrew Scriptures, for example, offer "An eye for an eye and a tooth for a tooth." The Christian Scriptures add "Turn the other cheek." A bumper sticker reads "Don't get mad, get even." Our feel-good culture sings "Don't worry, be happy!" A spouse tells us "You're just making a mountain out of a molehill." Relatives whisper "You're too sensitive." Friends advise "Don't take it so hard." The younger generation hoots "Get a life!" We wonder if perhaps we are imagining our own experiences of pain and alienation, and should just move on with life.

We are left with conflicting and confusing messages about forgiveness. At times, it seems, forgiveness does not enter the picture at all because reality is ignored. We seem limited to two options: get even or pretend the offense never happened.

Exercise

The purpose of this exercise is to bring to mind your own thoughts and opinions about forgiveness. Some of what you have learned is helpful, some is not. In your journal, make three lists about forgiveness.

First, list what your *personal experiences* have taught you about forgiveness. A helpful way to begin is with the sentence, "Forgiveness is
_____."

Next, make a list of what you learned about forgiveness from your *religious teachings*. What do you hear about forgiveness from the pulpit? from doctrines? from religious rituals? What "shoulds" and "oughts" do you associate with forgiveness?

Now make a third list of all the *cultural messages* you have heard about forgiveness. For example, what do you hear about forgiveness from movies? from television programs? from contemporary literature? from your family? When you were growing up, what were you taught to do when you were hurt? What do the sciences of psychology and sociology say about forgiveness?

For further reflection: Which messages about forgiveness have been helpful to you? Which messages have hindered your ability or willingness to forgive? What are some of your insights?

AN EXTRAORDINARY MOMENT OF GRACE

The January 9, 1984 cover of *Time* magazine grabbed the attention of the world. It was a picture of Pope John Paul II and his accused would-be assassin, Mehmet Ale Agca. The images were vivid. In a barren cell with white walls, the pope "held the hand that held the gun that was meant to kill him," and the caption across the photograph read "WHY FORGIVE? The Pope Pardons the Gunman."

Other pictures portrayed the two men sitting face to face on metal chairs in front of a radiator. Their knees appeared to be no more that twelve inches apart. One man wore a sweater, jeans, and shoes without laces; the other wore white robes and a white skull cap. There was a cot in the corner of the cell and bars on the high windows.

The article reported that after the two men spoke in whispers for twenty-one minutes, the pope emerged from the meeting and said, "I forgave him as a brother."

It had been over three years since the attempted murder in St. Peter's Square. The article described the pope's prison visit as "an extraordinary moment of grace," "violence transformed."

There are several lessons we can learn from this event, lessons crucial to understanding what forgiveness is and what it is not.

Note that the pope said, "I forgave him as a brother." He did not say that it is okay to go around shooting at popes or anyone else. Also note that the pope forgave the accused as a "brother," but he did not return the gun to the man. Finally, this act of forgiveness was offered for all the world to see *and* the accused remains behind bars.

This story suggests that forgiveness is many things but it is *not* approval. It is *not* the immediate restoration of trust. It is *not* canceling consequences.

The story also suggests that we can offer forgiveness to those who do not ask for it and to those who perhaps do not even want it; forgiveness offered and refused is not forgiveness negated. It remains an act of forgiveness. Forgiveness certainly does not have to be as public as in the case of the pope. In fact, the one being forgiven need not even know, as in the case of deceased family members and friends.

We do not know what, if any, effect the pope's forgiveness had on the gunman. We do know that forgiveness makes change possible, but that change first comes from within ourselves, within our hearts, minds, and actions. Forgiveness is never offered to coerce or change the other person. The story of the pope highlights the fact that forgiveness takes time, sometimes years. Forgiveness is not an event; it is a process.

Our "To-be-Forgiven" List

If forgiveness is not approval of others' attitudes or behavior, then our "to-be-forgiven" list can include those people we think are "dead wrong." If forgiveness does not have to include trusting the offender, then those who have repeatedly broken promises to us can be added to our list. If forgiveness does not ignore logical consequences, then we can include on our list those offenders who must be held accountable for their behavior.

Forgiveness does not begin with "It's okay. Just forget it." It begins, as in the story of the pope, by going to our own prisons: those places of hurt and resentment that imprison us. Forgiveness involves facing the enemies of our hearts.

A few years ago, during Lent, I decided to practice forgiveness in earnest. I made a list of the people toward whom I held strong resentments, wrote each name on a separate sheet of paper, folded the papers, and put them in a jar on my desk. Every morning I took out a folded slip. This was to be the person I would try to forgive that day. There were many days when the name I saw on the paper was too much to tackle, so I would quickly drop that name back into the jar and draw another, hoping that the second name would be easier to deal with. Facing the enemies of our hearts takes courage.

Exercise

In your journal write your reactions and responses to what you have read about forgiveness as it is portrayed in the magazine article about the pope and his accused would-be assassin. What struck you as new? different? surprising? difficult?

For further reflection: Reread what you have written, and let your own experiences sift through your thoughts. What do these insights say about your understanding of forgiveness? How do they support and/or contradict your understanding of forgiveness?

Conclusion

All of us desperately want to be transformed by forgiveness. The problem is we have never known how to forgive because forgiveness is something different from what we have been led to believe. I will always remember the woman who blurted out, "I thought forgiveness meant I just had to take it!" No, forgiveness does not mean we "take it."

Prayer

Ever-present Guide to the Journey,

You have placed the desire for reconciliation deep within me,
and I have felt it tug at my heart.
You have invited me on this excursion
through the mysteries of forgiveness,
but I am timid and unsure.

Help me to clear my mind of conflicting messages
and to look at forgiveness in new ways, with an open mind.
Guide my memories in the directions I need to go,
to the people I need to remember,
the prisons I need to revisit.

Be with me like a flashlight in the darkness,
an umbrella in the rain.
Be light and shelter for my journey,
for you are the spirit of my comings and goings.

2

ALIENATION REVISITED

Forgiveness is a process involving action on our part. It is a journey that begins with the experience of alienation and moves toward reconciliation.

A PLACE CALLED ALIENATION

We are people of passion and commitment. We are people who want and need nurturing relationships. When this nurture is absent or diminished, we are in a place I call alienation.

Alienation is a fact of life and a part of all relationships: relationships with self, with others, and with God. When we become somehow disconnected from these relationships, we experience a sense of separateness.

We cannot begin the journey of forgiveness until we revisit these places of alienation in our lives. We begin with the pain of alienation that is part of the fabric of our daily lives. We simply cannot avoid feeling disconnected, but we can choose to recover and move through the pain.

EXPERIENCES OF ALIENATION

Alienation comes in many obvious—and not so obvious—forms. I use examples from my own life experience to demonstrate a few varieties.

Not belonging: I grew up in the Cajun country of Louisiana and met my husband in New Orleans. When we moved to his hometown outside New York City after we were married, I felt like I had landed on the moon. Ed's friends and family were welcoming, but I felt lost. The weather was too cold and the pace was too fast. I had a recurring nightmare that I would die in my car driving around Manhattan trying to find a parking place. I felt far from home and was often homesick for anything familiar. I felt alienated, like I did not belong.

Disillusionment: I have a degree in early childhood education and was excited about having children. When I was the mother of three sons under six years of age, I discovered that I was not the mother I had hoped to be. I could not close the door of the playroom at three o'clock each day as I had done in the classroom. At times I felt unsure of myself, alienated from my earlier expectations of motherhood.

Failed expectations: Then I was the mother of three teens, and they fired me from my job as an over-solicitous mom. It was a blow to my self-esteem. As my youngest son was leaving for college I asked him, "Did you have a happy childhood?" I had to know. He said that indeed he had, yet I remembered all the mistakes I'd made, mistakes I was certain I would never make.

We place expectations on others, often unconsciously. Children grow up and do not live out the dreams their parents had for them. Parents turn out to be less perfect than their children once believed. People simply fail to live up to the expectations of others. One definition of forgiveness I find helpful is "Forgiveness is removing my expectations from you."

Emotional alienation: Married couples change and grow over the years. Part of their growth as a couple involves periods of distance and alienation from each other, followed by negotiations of renewed closeness. In some relationships this is not possible; the distance becomes too great and the affective connection cannot be reestablished.

One of the reasons I married Ed was because he was so calm and easy going. As time went on, his calm began to feel like disinterest to me. I began to believe that he did not care enough to stick with an argument until an issue was resolved. There were periods when we passed like ships in the night. The lack of clear communication around conflict and caring produced feelings of alienation in both of us.

At our wedding we had heard the words "And the two shall become one." For years we battled over which one we would become. Ed and I laugh about this now, but molding a long-term marriage creates ongoing cycles of alienation and reconciliation.

Other family relationships can suffer alienation, sometimes from old, perhaps unknown, wounds. My father and my uncle, for example, barely spoke to each other for as long as I can remember. No one talked about this cold war silence, but it was rumored that my father borrowed a small sum of money from my uncle and my uncle told everyone. I imagine that my father, newly married to my mother, must have felt ashamed and embarrassed.

My mother and I also experienced periods of alienation. We simply did not communicate well and had a long history of misunderstandings. Things I said were heard and interpreted differently from what I intended, leaving me confused, tongue-tied, and angry. Finally I lost hope for a warm relationship with my mother, and I went away to college.

Social alienation: Friends drift away; relationships grow cold. I still do not know what came between another couple and ourselves a decade ago. They drifted away and we ceased to care. If a friendship is important we will make every effort to reconnect. If we cannot, we will mourn the loss and may never understand what went wrong.

Addictions: Years ago we had to deal with drug abuse in our family. Everyone was affected, and the family experienced anger, resentment, and fear that sometimes bordered on terror. Any and all addictions alienate.

Institutional alienation: We can feel alienated from our Church. For example, many of us want the Church to come into the modern world. Others long for the way things used to be when we had all the answers. We can feel alienated from our country, our society. The chaos caused by government scandals and competing ideologies naturally creates a climate of wariness and estrangement.

Spiritual alienation: In his best seller, *When Bad Things Happen to Good People*, Rabbi Harold S. Kushner asks the question that has confronted and confounded people since time began. He points to a universal truth: people can and do feel alienated from God. A child dies, a spouse finds someone else, a young mother gets breast cancer, a family's breadwinner gets fired, and we are left to face the darkness.

EXERCISE

The purpose of these exercises is not to rush to a hasty, and therefore false, enactment of forgiveness. The goal is to take a long and honest look at relationships that presently cause you pain. Give yourself the gift of quiet time with your journal. Let your memory guide you while you write your responses.

When have you felt alienated from yourself? Make a list of those situations in which you felt lost or unsure of yourself.

Who has hurt you? List the names of people from whom you feel or have felt alienated, the people you resent, the people you love to hate, the people who have taken you for granted, shamed you, or used you. It does not matter if the hurt was intentional or not, or if some of these people are deceased. In fact, you may have to forgive someone for dying and leaving you. This list is about you and your hurts and alienation. Do not second-guess your list.

Finally, when has God seemed absent from your life? When have you felt confident that you could have done a better job with your life than God was doing?

For further reflection: Understand that there is such a thing as healthy alienation. We need the space to think and sort things out, to calm our fears, to discover our needs and desires, to share our fears with a trusted friend. We need to stay with the experience of alienation until we have had time to explore this place of uncertainty and discover more clarity for ourselves.

Yet we are made for community. Therefore alienation, even when it is helpful in the long run, frightens us. We seek to make peace at any price to avoid the pain of separation. With this caution in mind, reread your answers to the questions. Is there anything or anyone you left out?

REACTIONS TO ALIENATION

Quite naturally, alienation causes reactions. These usually take form in three different areas: in our emotions, in our behaviors, and in our perceptions of people and circumstances.

Emotional reactions: We "feel" alienation; we become lonely, frightened, angry, insecure. I felt lonely in New York, for example. I longed for a place like Cheers, "where everybody knows your name." As a wife and mother I sometimes felt unsure of myself. Sometimes I have felt resentment and rage toward friends who have moved on. Grief and shame have reminded me of some of my shortcomings. I have also experienced a thirst for revenge and a sense of hopelessness toward those who have accused me of selfishness in my dealings with them.

Behavioral reactions: We cry, slam doors, pout, blow our stacks, pretend that nothing is wrong, gossip, rerun the events in our mind, see red at the mention of his or her name, fantasize about "getting even."

A change in perspective: This may include a change in how we see ourselves, the offender, and/or God. Sometimes we begin by assuming that something is wrong with us. *It is all my fault. I deserved what happened. I'm not a loving person.* At other times we see the offender as a no-good so and so, and we see God as being more malevolent than compassionate and caring.

EXERCISE

How have your experiences of alienation affected your emotions? What feelings have been stirred up? Look at the persons and situations that you listed in the previous exercise. Reenter each memory, and write your feeling words (one word descriptions) next to each.

How has alienation affected your behavior? Look back at these hurtful scenes, and observe how you reacted to them. Record your observations about yourself. What did you do?

How has alienation affected your thinking and perceptions? What did you think or say to yourself? What did you think of those who offended you before and after the event or events? Record these shifts in attitudes. Also record any changes in your own self-image and in your image of God.

For further reflection: Some people have caused us pain unintentionally and others have done so deliberately. We have misread certain situations and taken offense when none was meant. We have been victims of emotional or physical abuse, or both. We have been down on ourselves and down on God. We have bumped into the unfairness of life. All of these situations beg our attention because all of them take us to the place of alienation.

Do you see any patterns of alienation in your life? Do you see the same people or kinds of people causing problems for you over time? What kinds of situations cause you the most distress, hence alienation? How do you react overall to the alienation that you experience?

CONCLUSION

When we remember the painful places in our lives we usually relive the feelings. We sometimes regret our reactions. When we get stuck in alienation, we relive the event as if it happened yesterday. Over time we begin to build a case against ourselves, others, and/or God. We begin to mistrust life.

The only way out of alienation is through forgiveness. Forgiveness begins with me and not with the alleged offender. In other words, forgiveness does not depend on the offender's repentance. Forgiveness begins with my perceived loss and my felt experience of alienation.

You have begun. In this chapter you have revisited the pain and loss. You have identified some of the consequences, namely negative feelings, hurtful actions and reactions, and negative perceptions of others, self, and God. You are ready to move on, to examine ways to work with and through the pain and suffering of alienation.

PRAYER

Timeless, Eternal God of History,

You are within the warm bustle of relationships,
* where I easily recognize your face*
* in the faces of those I love.*
You are within the cold, still seasons of alienation,
* where I often do not recognize or even sense*
* your presence.*

Deliver me from the denial of painful memories
* because I feel afraid and hateful and confused.*
Do not let me run from the negative actions and thoughts
* which I am ashamed to admit are a part of me.*

Lead me to embrace my experiences of betrayal.
* Refresh my memory with clarity.*
Anoint my confession with honesty.
I pray through the One
* whose betrayal and death led to resurrection,*
* God, my Presence and Strength for all Seasons.*

3

A PATH THROUGH THE PAIN

B y now we realize that forgiveness is not simply the making or accepting of an apology. It is not the old "let bygones be bygones" or "offering it up" approach. Although there is some truth in each of these actions, we know from the depths of personal experience that there is more; there *has* to be more.

FORGIVENESS AND RESENTMENT

Betty was a baptized Lutheran who was married in the Catholic faith. She and her husband had two daughters who were baptized in the Catholic faith as well, but the family did not attend church regularly for many years. When her older daughter, Suzanne, was a senior in high school and preparing for college, Betty and her family began to attend Mass at the local Catholic parish. After Suzanne went away to college that fall, the family remained active in the life of the parish.

The following spring, Suzanne was injured in a freak automobile accident. She lay in a coma for days. There was a young man, another car accident victim, also clinging to life in the hospital's intensive care unit. The two families consoled each other in the ICU waiting room. Both young people died.

With time, Suzanne's mother decided to join the Catholic Church. The young man's grandmother, a Catholic, stopped going to church after her grandson's death. Both women shared the same tragic experience, but each responded differently.

These two individuals must have struggled with questions that have no answers and sought meaning where only confusion is to be found. One was able to come through the grief and anger; the other was not. What made the difference? Forgiveness.

When senseless tragedy strikes us we want to strike back; we seek someone or something to blame. In our American culture, this often takes the form of lawsuits. When we can't find someone or something to blame and hold responsible, we turn to God. We resent God; we blame God.

The grandmother could not get past her need to blame. She believed that God let her down, so she walked away. Betty, on the other hand, moved beyond this very human tendency to place blame and cling to resentment. Forgiveness made the difference between the two responses, because forgiveness always draws us beyond resentments and defuses blame.

The choice between resentment and forgiveness affects our human relationships as well. When my husband and I were newly married and lived on the East Coast in the early sixties, scandal and divorce were rare. There was, however, an incident that upset everyone.

Carol, a married woman with three young children, discovered that her husband was having an affair with her best friend. The small town gossip mills worked overtime. To make matters worse, the affair seems to have been aided by mutual friends.

Carol was devastated. For a long time she raged at anyone who would listen; she was inconsolable. Eventually the couple divorced, and Carol's former husband married her former best friend. Carol was jilted by both.

We moved away and lost track of Carol. Years later, however, I saw her when we returned to visit relatives. I was stunned. Carol was beautiful. I expected to see a person whose face was chiseled by years of bitterness, but I saw no bitterness. She had some gray hair and a few wrinkles, but she looked lovely and peaceful. How did she get past the rage and shame? Forgiveness.

Carol used her anger to move her into and through healing. She turned her rage into anger and her anger into positive energy. She sought counseling, joined a support group, and began to put her life back together.

Carol journeyed to a place of inner reconciliation without the offender's active participation in her life. We do not know how her journey of forgiveness affected her former husband, but we do know that any act of forgiveness breaks the negative cycle of criticism and blame.

With time, people ceased to talk about Carol as the jilted woman, presumably because she ceased wearing the label. She no longer allowed her former husband's actions to define who she was. "The jilted woman" is no longer the title of her biography, but is only one chapter in the book.

Sometimes the pain comes into our hearts and families from the outside world. A few years ago I was selected for jury duty in a criminal case. Jury candidates for these trials are routinely asked, "Have you or any member of your family ever been the victim of a violent crime?" An elderly African-American man replied, "Yes. My son was murdered." He was selected for the jury as well.

One day during lunch, I asked the man how he was able to come to terms with the murder of his child. He told me that it had taken some time, but "The police did a good job," he said. "They were good to my family." That's all he said.

The man's words spoke of a gentle acceptance. He seemed to have made peace with the tragedy, but how? I sensed that he had taken the journey of forgiveness and discovered the peace that reconciliation can bring. He turned his attention from mentally replaying the horrible events of the murder to focusing on the kindness the police offered in the midst of his pain. He saw and spoke of what was given rather than what was taken away.

These are only a few stories of people whose lives were broken and later transformed. None of them wished or dreamed that the drama of their lives would be played out in these particular ways. No doubt, they still experience times of regret or sorrow. Yet, they have survived; in fact, they have done more than survive. The very real and tragic moments in their life histories are not being forgotten; they are being transformed. They chose to forgive and to move on with living.

EXERCISE

Recall a time in your life when you were able to move beyond hurt. In your journal describe your feelings, reactions, and perceptions, both before and after your experience of pain and alienation.

For further reflection: How and why were you able to forgive? What were the factors contributing to forgiveness? Did you consider this an experience of forgiveness at the time? Why, do you think, is it an experience of forgiveness now?

Toward Reconciliation

When we look around for new paths through our brokenness we must look beyond easy fixes. We do not want to be stuck in overt resentments or covert anger. We do not want to become slaves to a biased way of thinking that blames everyone for our pain. Rather we want to be transformed beyond these prisons.

Scripture scholars tell us that when the writers of the Bible spoke of the reality of lives transformed, they used three different words: the Hebrew words *shuv* and *niham* and the Greek word *metanoeo*.

Shuv means "to turn or return." Our word "conversion" expresses this reality. We speak of a "conversion of heart" when our hearts soften and turn to God. *Niham* means "to repent and be sorry." Our word "repentance" captures the meaning. We are to repent our actions and reform our lives. *Metanoeo* means "to change one's mind." In English we use the word "metanoia," which is a change in thinking, perceiving, or believing.

The words from the prophet Joel, "Return to me with your whole heart" (2:12) and from the evangelist, Mark, "Repent, and believe in the gospel" (1:15) speak of this transformation. We are called to a change of heart, a change of actions, and a change of perception. This is the path we must walk if we are to be transformed and made whole again. This is our path through alienation, brokenness, and pain.

A change of heart: We begin by revisiting our resentments and getting in touch with our feelings. This means working with those active resentments—those resentments that we almost enjoy harboring. These are the barriers that block all other emotions from our consciousness. Only when we revisit these parts of our broken hearts can we know and name our feelings and begin to grieve.

Betty, the woman who became a Catholic after her child died, was able to do this. She moved beyond the resentment of her eldest child being cruelly snatched away when life promised so much. She got past blaming and resenting God and others for life and death. She talked about how it

32

felt to be overwhelmed with loss. She was not afraid of her feelings, and shed many tears in the process.

A change of actions: A change of actions forces us to look at hidden anger. Alienation paralyzes us. Not only do resentments freeze over so we cannot feel and grieve, anger freezes over into rage and we cannot act. Instead we get stuck in certain reactions that we repeat even when they do not offer relief. We all know people who have told the same story of woe for years; they almost seem to enjoy reliving their tragedy. They are caught up in repetitive reactions that offer no relief.

Carol, whose husband left her for her best friend, got in touch with her anger. Her behavior may have been driven by blind rage at first, but somewhere along the way she stopped reacting. She befriended her anger, took energy from it, and let it move her to constructive action. Gradually, Carol was able to not only forgive her husband but herself as well, because forgiveness of others always invites forgiveness of self.

Forgiveness, of course, does not translate into approval of what was done, and it does not erase guilt. Rather, forgiveness draws us beyond the experience of shame. Remember this distinction: guilt says the action is flawed; shame says the person is flawed. Carol accepted the guilt that said she, too, had made mistakes that contributed to the flawed relationship, but she did not accept the shame that said she was a flawed human being because of her mistakes.

For Carol, renewed self-respect gradually replaced public humiliation. That is why she looked so peaceful. That is what forgiveness does for us.

A change of perceptions: When we are in pain we can experience frozen feelings and frozen, repetitive reactions. We can also get stuck in how we perceive the situation and the people involved. We freeze the event in our mind's eye and lose sight of the bigger picture. We make the offender the enemy.

The gentleman on the jury was able to see the bigger picture. When he talked about his son's murder he told his story in that curious way. "The police did a good job. They were good to my family." He could have talked about those who committed the murder. He could have talked about blame. His words could have cut with the sharp edge of bitterness. Instead the man spoke of kindness and resolution. Forgiveness allowed him—as it will us—to see things that are not immediately apparent, like goodness in the midst of evil.

EXERCISE

Reread your responses to the previous exercise. Try to further pinpoint how you were able to forgive. Did you move beyond resentments? How? Did you befriend your anger? How? Were you able to see a different perspective that freed you? What was that new perspective? What caused this change? If you were unable to forgive, what was and is blocking this in you?

For further reflection: Begin to compose a list of definitions of forgiveness as you understand it so far. Compare this with the first exercise in chapter 1: the messages you learned about forgiveness from life, religious teachings, and the culture. (See page 18.) What does forgiveness have to do with resentment? with blame? with guilt? with shame and embarrassment? What part do perceptions about others and self play in the act of forgiveness?

CONCLUSION

We have explored the problem of separation. We have focused on alienation and our reactions to the hurt it causes. We have explored what forgiveness is and what it is not. We have learned that the path through the pain of alienation means getting in touch with how we feel, how we act and react, and how we think and perceive. We realize that forgiveness begins with ourselves. It is a decision that involves changes in us; it does not depend on changes in the offender.

We have looked at personal stories of forgiveness and have seen that forgiveness does not have to be reciprocal to be authentic. It is not necessarily a two-way street. Forgiveness is first something we do for ourselves. It is something we *must* do if we are to become whole again.

These personal stories also demonstrate that forgiveness is neither other-dependent nor self-righteousness: "I forgive you even though I know you are wrong and I am right." The people we read about did not "stoop" to forgive, or "settle" for forgiveness. If they had, their own healing would have come to a standstill.

In part 2 you will walk carefully through each of the three changes involved in forgiveness and reconciliation: changes in feelings, changes in actions, and changes in perceptions. You will begin by looking at resentments, blame, and grief (chapter 4), move to consider rage and anger and anger's role in making change (chapter 5), and conclude with an examination of your perceptions and the role your imagination plays in the healing process (chapter 6).

PRAYER

Inviting, Coaxing God,

You call, and I hear your invitation
to return, to repent, to believe.
But what if I discover I am too set in my ways,
and resist change and growth?

You summon, and I stand hesitant,
a mixture of excitement and nervousness.
What if I find out that deep down
I don't want to forgive an old rival?

Give me the desire to try in spite of my misgivings.
Get tough with me about my cherished resentments.
Unlock my heart
and coax me out of the familiar smugness
of righteous indignation.

Anoint me with the courage to hold on and the boldness to let go
as I begin in earnest the work of forgiveness.
Be persistent with me, O God.

PART II
FORGIVENESS

4

UNCOVERING RESENTMENT

Resentment is like Pandora's box. It is an emotionally charged container filled with all sorts of painful feelings and negative images of the offender. We would like to keep the lid closed but it keeps flying open, letting loose all sorts of fury and chaos.

It is not so much that we have resentments but rather that resentments have us—and sometimes we actually find some kind of self-serving satisfaction in that. Inspector Javert spent years tracking Jean Valjean in *Les Miserables*, consumed with resentment and self-righteousness. Cinderella's sisters looked upon her with envy and resentment, and punished her with insults and isolation. Cain resented Abel and took him out into the fields and murdered him.

The prophet of God calls to us, "Return to me with your whole heart" (Joel 2:12). The psalmist sings "A clean heart create for me, God" (51:12). We are invited to look into our hearts to uncover resentments lurking there. We are invited to allow our hardened hearts to be changed into hearts of fleshy feelings.

THE HEARTACHE OF RESENTMENT

Resentment is first of all a heart problem. Forgiveness would be easy if the offender had a change of heart and came to us on bended knee, remorseful and contrite. Heart to heart, we would be reconciled and our wounds would mend. Unfortunately life is seldom like this.

Forgiveness is difficult when the offender is unaware of our pain. It is even more difficult when the offender does not think any wrong was committed, or could care less. Whatever the circumstances, forgiveness is always possible. It begins with the decision to revisit resentments.

EXERCISE

This is a three-part exercise that I call "writing lines." Take care to write the sentences exactly as instructed. We will examine the entire exercise after it's completed. I tell workshop participants to trust the process and just do it.

First: Return to your list of those who have hurt you. (See page 25.) Choose one person toward whom you still harbor active, negative feelings and thoughts because of something he or she did to *you*, not someone else. In your journal complete this sentence at least four times, naming no less than four different reasons for your resentment. It is important to be specific about the actions that triggered your distress.

(Name the person), I resent you because you (name the specific action).

When I first did this exercise I chose to look at resentments I still had toward my mother who died in 1992. I wrote:

1. *Mother*, I resent you because you *pushed me to achieve.*
2. *Mother*, I resent you because you *argued with Dad a lot.*
3. *Mother*, I resent you because you *blamed me for your unhappiness.*
4. *Mother*, I resent you because you *punished me with angry silence.*

Second: Repeat the sentences exactly as you just wrote them, but change the word "resent" to "appreciate." It's important to change only the word "resent," and to change it to "appreciate," even if the sentiment sounds false. Notice where you feel a strong reaction. I wrote:

1. Mother, I *appreciate* you because you pushed me to achieve.
2. Mother, I *appreciate* you because you argued with Dad a lot.
3. Mother, I *appreciate* you because you blamed me for your unhappiness.
4. Mother, I *appreciate* you because you punished me with angry silence.

Third: Again, repeat the sentences but with another variation. Remove all references to the offender and focus only on the actions. "I" replaces "you" as the subject of your sentences. I wrote:

1. *I* pushed me to achieve.
2. *I* argued with Dad a lot.
3. *I* blamed me for your unhappiness.
4. *I* punished me with angry silence.

When you finish writing to your satisfaction, return to your original four sentences and read them slowly and out loud. Listen carefully to each thought. Do the same with the second set of sentences and the third set of sentences.

For further reflection: Not all of what you wrote will fit your experience, but most of the sentences have insights to offer. For example, which sentences trigger feelings such as hot anger or cool relief? Which sentences offer new insights? Where do you say, "Aha"? Where do you feel resistance or confusion?

Which of your specific actions can you see more clearly now? What hidden appreciations did you uncover within the resentments? What actions did you discover you could actually own in the third section of the exercise? What new insights did you discover?

Owning Up

Resentments are often vague and free-floating. To capture them we must get very specific. When I began to name the specific actions that triggered my resentments toward my mother, I discovered some surprises. Writing the sentences in the previous exercise confirmed for me that my mother did indeed push me to achieve, but I began to realize that she was like all parents. She wanted to take pride in her offspring. At times, I resisted her pushing. Arguments followed and alienation set in. There was reason for my resentment.

Yet, I have to admit that my mother's investment in my life contributed greatly to the person I am today. Although I resented the pressure she applied at the time, today I appreciate the fruit of her attention and efforts. Being pushed was not all bad, and in fact, I've come to realize that the pressure I experienced was not all my mother's doing. I pushed myself, often to the point of being overextended. I have to own my part of the strained relationship.

Relishing Resentment

There are payoffs hidden within resentments. We relish and nurse our resentments because we get something out of them. We can resent others because we think they are wrong and we are right, giving us a sense of self-righteousness, which in turn makes us feel superior.

The arsenal of resentment can also help us garner sympathy from third parties who agree with us. When we hear ourselves say he or she "always" or "never," we are voicing resentment, exaggerating our case, and soliciting support.

Resentment creates a negative energy that keeps us vigilant. When we see the offender at a family gathering, we watch him or her out of the corner of our eye. We want to know what he or she is up to. We want to gather more evidence.

Resentment is a way to remain connected to the offender. In fact, it may be all we have left. Long after the divorce, we hear the offended party talking about the "ex" as if it happened yesterday. We remain connected through the negative energy of resentment.

Resentment also allows us to project onto the offender what we do not like in ourselves. We complain about the neighbor who gossips about us without realizing that we are—*gossiping about the neighbor!*

Sometimes resentment is the only thing we can feel. Yet, it isn't exactly a feeling; it's more like a lump, like a dish of rotting stew too long forgotten in the rear of the refrigerator. We do not feel sorrow or pain, we feel a lump of resentment. But at least we feel something.

Sometimes we are too ashamed to admit that we are envious of someone, so we resent the person instead. We resent the person's wealth, good luck, or whatever we wish we had. Sometimes the resentment toward the offender is so old and so familiar that we cannot imagine life without it; we've almost come to find it entertaining. In truth, it is scary to let go of something we have nurtured with all our hearts for a very long time.

THE CORE OF RESENTMENT

I resented my mother because she blamed me for her unhappiness; I believed this for years. It was one of those unexamined resentments. Then, when I wrote, "*I* blamed me," I had one of those life-changing "aha" moments.

Suddenly I realized the truth: I had blamed myself. I believed that I must have done something to make my mother unhappy. As a child I thought as a child: "If I do everything right, then everyone will be happy. If anyone becomes unhappy, it will be because I did something wrong." I do not think my mother blamed me at all. I think I projected my self-blame onto her. I turned it all around, and this childish belief lasted, unexamined, into adulthood.

Blame offers us payoffs. When we hold the other person responsible, we don't have to look at ourselves. Blame keeps us focused outside ourselves, blocks our real feelings, and prevents us from taking charge of our own lives. Blame is the core of resentment.

Families easily play the blame game. Family members take emotional sides when they judge that another member of the family is unfair. Resentments build and, over time, the family creates its black sheep, its scapegoat. Stories of who did what and who is to blame become part of the family myth.

When we blame others for our pain we hold them responsible for more than just the offense. We make them responsible for our emotional reactions to the offense: "You hurt my feelings. You are to blame. You made me feel bad." Yet, no one makes us "feel." When we understand this, we stop the blaming habit. We stop handing out free guilt trips. We give up trying to control others through blame.

The fact is, we are not responsible for others' reactions and they are not responsible for ours. We are not to blame for their feelings, and they are not to blame for ours. We can hold the other person accountable for his or her actions. We can even impose consequences. We can thoroughly disapprove of what was said or done, and we can even withhold trust. This is all very different from blaming. This is a difficult concept to grasp because most of us have been taught that we can and should keep others happy.

I resented my mother because it seemed to me that she was always arguing with my father. Today I realize that my father must have been part of the arguments too. I know from experience that couples argue and that this is healthy. Yet for years I secretly sided with my father and blamed my mother. I had it all wrong.

Getting in touch with our feelings, however, is the first step toward better understanding our resentments and tendencies to blame. The late Father Lawrence Jenco was held captive in Lebanon for several years. After his release he said in an interview, "Until we allow ourselves to feel the pain it is unlikely an act of forgiveness will be genuine." Forgiveness insists that we feel our feelings.

Exercise

Return to the four specific resentments that you listed in the first part of the previous exercise. Choose two resentments that are most alive and hold the most negative energy for you right now.

Make a list of the feelings within each resentment. Give names to these feelings. (You may want to refer to your list of feelings from page 26.) Describe the feelings in terms of images that convey how your body feels ("like the weight of the world is on my shoulders," "like a rug has been pulled out from under me"), and in terms of bodily sensations ("heavy," "weighted down," "shaken up," "tense," "nauseated").

I selected to work with my resentment over my mother pushing me to achieve and punishing me with angry silence. I wrote:

1. When you pushed me to achieve I often felt nervous, like my insides were shaking. I felt tremendous pressure when you nagged me to vote for myself to win a graduation award. I felt scared I wouldn't win and would disappoint you. Scared is a tense feeling, like I'm holding my breath and sucking my

stomach in. Sometimes I felt so angry I thought I would explode.
I wanted to shout at you and run away.

2. When you punished me with your angry silences I felt empty
and defeated, drained of energy. After Dad's funeral I remember
discussing the estate. I don't know what happened but suddenly
you turned. When I touched your arm and tried to talk, you
jerked away and refused to speak to me for the next few days. I
felt lonely and hollow like there was nothing to me. It was like
I was not even there, the Invisible Girl. It hurt. I ached like I had
the flu. I wanted to cry and never stop.

Now complete the exercise using your two resentments and describing
your feelings:

When you (name the action) I felt (describe your feelings).

You may return to this exercise often, adding more feelings and descriptions as you become aware of them.

For further reflection: Which feelings are the most difficult for you? Which
are the most fearful? Why?

GRIEF

Once we get in touch with our feelings and remove some of the blame,
we make significant progress in the forgiving process. At this point, however, we must grieve. When we take responsibility for our own reactions
and feelings, when we look within and fully feel our pain and our sorrow,
we grieve.

For example, I felt deep sadness when a good friend became increas-
ingly distant. I met her for lunch one day and asked if I had done anything
to offend her. She said that I had not, but nothing I said that day or over the
next several months restored the warmth we had shared.

I felt like I had been punched in the stomach. I was confused. How dare
her! I felt embarrassed. Maybe I had done something and she no longer
wanted to bother with me. I resented her for a long time and blamed her
for refusing to talk things through. I blamed myself for some unknown
sin. We drifted apart.

Several years later I made a retreat and was invited to reflect on the losses I had experienced over the years. It was then that I was able to see that the end of that friendship was a real loss for me. I had lost a good friend, someone I could talk with. I missed our stimulating conversations, our shopping trips, our exchanges of family news. I began to name and accept all this and to move through the resentment and blame. I began to grieve the loss of this relationship.

During this time, painful feelings returned to me. A familiar sadness weighed down on my chest and ebbed and flowed. Gradually, the feelings became less intense and less frequent. In the process I forgave my friend, I forgave myself, and I moved on. Today I remember her and our times together with fondness. I realize that I could not remember our good times until I had worked through forgiveness. Now I am thankful we were friends at least for a while. If I ever see her again I will tell her so.

Unfortunately, most of us are afraid of the pain of loss so we try to avoid facing our losses and experiencing grief. C. S. Lewis wrote *A Grief Observed* (The Seabury Press, 1961) following the death of his wife, Joy. The book begins, "No one ever told me that grief felt so like fear." Perhaps the fear we feel is really the beginning of the grief process that is essential to the journey of forgiveness.

EXERCISE

In this exercise you will be writing about the losses and regrets in your relationship with the offender. I wrote:

Mother, when I think of you I remember some good times and feel a deep sadness that they can be no more. I enjoyed taking you shopping. I smile when I remember how well you bore my near automobile misses when I drove us around Ireland. I loved sharing recipes with you. I remember how I admired your long manicured fingernails when I was a child. I miss your wisdom.

Yet some resentments linger. I know that the angry, silent treatments were your way of handling conflict, yet they always spoke volumes to me. Early on I took them to mean that you could not bear to speak to me. I was not worthy of conversation.

I still feel some anger and disappointment, regrets and doubts. Regret tastes like bitter medicine. I choke on it. I have regrets about our relationship. I wish it had been different. I wish we had been closer, but I don't think I knew how to accomplish that. Doubts remain. Sometimes I wonder if you really cared for me. Did I tell you I loved you? I wonder if you really knew. I wonder if you ever forgave me for whatever I did that made you angry and silent.

Anger lingers even now. I still have moments when I want to shout at you (and I do). I still want to change you into a better mother than you were.

I grieve for what we did not have. I wish we could have been more honest with one another. I grieve for what can never be made right. I miss not having a mother. I wish you could have met your great-grandchildren and seen me as a grandmother.

Give yourself all the time you need for this exercise. You may want to make a list or write this exercise as a letter. What do you miss about the offender? about the relationship? What regrets or doubts still linger?

For further reflection: How do you feel when you remember the losses and the regrets of the past? When a feeling surfaces, grab it before it hides. Repeat over and over the name of your strongest feeling. Do this out loud. Exaggerate it by naming related feelings that amplify it. Act it out. Punch a pillow or write the feeling many times, pressing the pen to the paper. Do this with each of the other feelings you described until you can say them easily.

CONCLUSION

Resentment is one of the roadblocks to forgiveness. Resentment resides in a secluded corner of the heart where we hide feelings too painful to feel and too scary to acknowledge. All of these feelings go by one common name: "resentment."

The journey of forgiveness invites us to be very specific about the things we resent and about the feelings we have suppressed. We must allow the feelings to do their work in the process of forgiveness: to help us grieve through the pain of alienation.

Forgiveness involves feeling all of your feelings. It is a grieving process. You must grieve that which you have lost in your relationships. Forgiveness is not an eraser. It is not a solution. You cannot pretend the past did not happen. You cannot return and solve the problems of the past. Grieving, however, will allow you, someday, to remember the past without reliving the feelings. Grief is one of the paths through forgiveness. There are no shortcuts.

PRAYER

Creator of Human Drama,

You call forth my feelings
* and then offer yourself as a pin cushion for those that prick.*
You are like a sponge
* and absorb all my losses when I can no longer bear their pain.*

Help me to always feel all of my feelings.
* Sharpen them until I am compelled to acknowledge*
* and name them.*
Lead me gently now to focus on my feelings of anger.
* Come close as I explore this remarkable source of*
* life's energy.*

Teach me the ways of passion,
* lead me to the depths of new discoveries.*
Passionate God, you demand a passionate response.

5
DISCOVERING ANGER

I n the previous chapter the prophet Joel reminds us of God's call: "Return to me" (2:12). Gently, we returned to those places in our lives where our hearts had been broken. We took a critical look at our resentments and the reasons behind them, named and described our painful feelings, and remembered and grieved our losses.

Now the gospel invites, "Repent, and believe in the gospel" (Mark 1:15). "Repent," like the words "return to me," is a call for change. Forgiveness is about a change or conversion of heart. It is also, as we just experienced, about a change or repentance of actions.

THE EMOTIONAL SEESAW

When we are hurt by another person we get angry. Anger is a natural response, but most of us do not believe this. Our families of origin, our religious backgrounds, and the "shoulds" and "oughts" of our culture conspire to stamp out anger.

Our culture harbors an enduring prejudice about anger: avoid it. "Come on, kiss and make up." "Don't take it so hard." "Calm down." These are but a few of the ready-made answers to anger that offer advice on how to act and how not to act when we have been hurt.

The truth is, we are afraid of anger. For example, we're afraid to talk about anger. We veil it with words like "annoyed," "upset," or "disappointed." We're afraid to feel anger. What if it gets out of hand and we blow up? What if it leads to rage and violence?

But anger cannot—will not—be denied. When we are hurt, we experience anger. It is as natural as feeling pleasure when we have been praised. The anger we feel, however, can take two directions. It can go up or down. It can become hot or cold. Anger can heat up into rage or cool down into sadness and depression.

Some of us quickly mask our gut feeling of anger with politeness. Some of us become enraged and use our anger to bear down on everything and everyone in our path, like the glaring headlights of an oncoming semitruck. Some of us simmer and steep as silently as tea brews in a teapot. Some of us hurl verbal attacks through the air with the precision of an Olympic javelin thrower. Some of us kick the dog or eat everything in sight. Some of us cry and pout. I used to slam doors.

None of these responses are honest. They are seesaw reactions because they do not deal directly with the anger. One of the reasons we cannot forgive is because we cannot clearly express our anger or even admit it. We overreact or underreact rather than act. We get stuck in habitual reactions of either magnifying or diminishing our anger. Some of us swing back and forth between the two extremes, always arriving at the same old place: either swallowing anger whole or spewing it all over everyone else.

Unexpressed or overexpressed anger denies authentic anger the opportunity to do its work, and the work of anger is to lead us to truth and change. We begin by claiming it.

EXERCISE

This is a two-part exercise. Return to the two specific resentments you wrestled with in the last chapter. (See page 44.) You are going to continue writing lines, but with another variation.

First: In the original writing-lines exercise on page 40, you wrote "(Name the person), I resent you because you (name the specific action)." Use this same pattern for the two specific resentments you are working on (see page 45), but replace the word "resent" with "am angry at." I originally wrote, "Mother, I resent you because you pushed me to achieve" and "Mother, I resent you because you punished me with angry silence." My rewritten sentences read, "Mother, I *am angry at* you because you pushed me to achieve" and "Mother, I *am angry at* you because you punished me with angry silence."

The structure you will use for your sentence is: "(Name the person), I am angry at you because you (name the specific action)."

Second: Write the sentences again, replacing "am angry at" with "demand that you stop." I wrote, "Mother, I demand that you stop pushing me to achieve!" and "Mother, I demand that you stop punishing me with angry silence!"

The structure you will use for your sentence is: "(Name the person), I demand that you stop (name the specific action)."

For further reflection: Read your list aloud with verbal emphasis on your anger. You may even shake your fist in the air each time you say the word "angry." You may want to stand up, stomp your foot, raise your voice, and shout when you "demand."

What sensations do you feel in your body as you claim your anger? How does it feel to "put your foot down"?

THE PROTEST OF ANGER

We get angry when our best attempts at living our own lives are frustrated. This first comes to light in the two-year-old. The task for this age is to begin to separate from the caretakers, and of course, toddlers take this task very seriously. All attempts to rein in these budding explorers are met with angry frustration. All questions and suggestions are met with one word: "No!"

Ignoring anger is impossible. It simply appears in another form. We experience physical aches, ulcers, depression, all sorts of illnesses when we ignore anger.

Claiming anger helps us recover this basic ability to say "no." It moves us to set boundaries and to acknowledge what we will and will not tolerate in our relations with others. Saying "no" helps us reclaim self-respect. It's like a protest against someone standing on our foot. We have to say "Ouch!" or the person will just stand there out of ignorance or malice. To say nothing and smile politely is to allow the pain to continue or, worse, to be a partner in an abusive situation.

Anger says, "The truth is you're standing on my foot. It hurts and I demand that you stop." Anger is a protest against an unacceptable situation. We need to reclaim permission to feel anger and to develop skills to express anger responsibly.

NAMING THE ISSUES

We get angry when we perceive diminishment. We recognize that our own needs, rights, and self-esteem—or that of others—are being ignored or violated. Anger gives us the energy we need to address injustices. "What do I need to get angry at today?" is a good question for personal reflection.

Several years ago I lead the rehearsal for the Easter Vigil service at my parish. After I dismissed the group, a few people lingered to ask me some last-minute questions. While I reviewed details with them, my husband approached me, stopped the conversation in progress, and told me that he was going to a department store to pick up the chest we had been thinking about buying. He wanted to know what I thought about that.

I was so taken aback by the interruption that I couldn't think straight. I told him that I didn't know and went on talking. By the time I got home I was seething.

I walked around the house mumbling and grumbling, rehearsing everything I wanted to say to Ed when he got home: "You interrupted me. You always interrupt me! You were rude, darn it!

It was like I was suddenly thrown a curve ball and I didn't even know I was in the game. "You made me lose my train of thought. I hate being interrupted, especially when I'm at my job! Why did you do that?!" I was furious, enraged.

By the time Ed got home—with the chest, I might add—I had begun to ask myself why this incident bothered me so much. I started to realize that for me the issue was one of self-diminishment. I had been "at the office" so to speak, and Ed's interruption had ignored what I was doing. It was as if my job was not all that important. I had felt embarrassed by his intrusion, and I was angry at him for intruding.

I could have lapsed into pouting; I could have exploded into rage. I have done both over the years, I am sorry to say. That time, however, I was able to name my issues and spell them out for Ed. He apologized and said that the minute the words were out of his mouth he regretted them. The incident certainly could have gone the other way, with both of us exchanging accusations and feeling hurt and misunderstood.

Anger is about specifics. It helps us sort out the issues. Rage, on the other hand, is about generalities. It is both unfocused and undisciplined. Rage is a fury, a tornado of feelings and grievances that swirl about and suck us into its whirlwind. In the midst of rage, we lose touch with reality. Rage punches (or murders) the person standing on our foot. When we name the issues for ourselves, we convert rage into anger.

We speak rage in "you" statements: "*You* interrupted me. *You* embarrassed me. *You* made me angry." We speak anger in "I" statements: "*I* didn't like what you did. *I* felt embarrassed. *I* value my job. *I* don't want you to interrupt me. *I* intend to get angry if it happens again."

Anger is a tool to get to the truth, *my* truth. It points me to the issue beneath the issue, the personal issue beneath the issue of the offender's actions.

EXERCISE

Return to your two specific resentments against the offender. Explore how the offender's actions specifically affected you. I wrote:

Mother, when you pushed me to achieve I think you had worthy goals in mind for me, but being first in the class wasn't what I really wanted for myself. I wanted to have more free time. Striving to win all the awards put me in competition with some of my friends.

I often felt uncomfortable. Sometimes I was shunned by other students. I pushed myself because I thought I had to please you, and I wanted to please you. Often it was your agenda and not mine that I was living. Often it was your dreams I was being asked to fulfill. My desire to chase after some of my own dreams took second place. Sometimes I wanted to shout, "Whose life is this anyhow?"

Mother, when you ignored me with angry silence I was cut off. My feeble attempts to make up were rarely responded to. I had no way to communicate with you. I never knew what you were thinking. Sometimes I didn't even know why you were angry, what I had done. Each time it would blow over, but it seems nothing was ever resolved. I don't think we really knew one another. I was scared to talk to you. As a young girl, my needs for a relationship with you were not met.

In your own writing, you may want to consider how you were diminished by the offender's actions: What about you was ignored or denied? What was taken away from you? What parts of yourself did you lose?

For further reflection: What insights can you identify? Notice how naming your diminishments helps you refocus your attention. Notice how some issues are more important to you than others. Some are worth fighting for; others are secondary. What is important to your self-esteem at age twenty may not be as important when you reach forty. The issues beneath long-held grievances may be outdated. Which issues are still important for you? Which are secondary or perhaps even unimportant today?

USING ANGER WELL

If we attend to it well, anger is a special source of energy. Anger can move us toward saying and doing our truth and getting our needs met. Anger can point us toward justice.

Great reformers, like Martin Luther King, Jr. and Mahatma Gandhi, are examples of people who used their anger toward injustice in the service of justice. They were passionate people. In the Bible we read about the anger of Moses and Jesus, even of Yahweh. It is anger for right action, a passion to speak truth.

Author Robert Bly describes the mood of some of the newer spirituality movements as "addicted to harmony," in which anger is neutralized and passion gives way to a kind of passivity. The goal of this kind of thinking is to release negative feelings—nothing more. Forgiveness is considered irrelevant. We see this in marriages when the spouses are too frightened to rock their boat of mediocrity. Instead of entering the hard work of sorting out the issues, they settle for the shallow payoffs of peaceful coexistence or a not-so-peaceful truce. Many even call this "forgiveness."

Abusive relationships often get caught in this same tendency to neutralize anger. The abused party repeatedly lets bygones be bygones in the face of each new promise of change on the part of the abuser. Yet, as long as physical or emotional abuse continues, there can be no authentic forgiveness. Anger can energize us for the task.

A number of years ago I was trying to have a conversation with one of my teenagers, but we were not communicating. He said some things that I did not appreciate, and I had a flash of anger. In response, I told him that I was not going to continue the conversation at that time because I respected myself too much to listen to his verbal abuse. I left the room.

My anger was a wake-up call. It allowed me to draw the line on what I would tolerate in the relationship with my son. Anger moved me to speak my truth, namely that I would not accept how I was being treated. The logical consequence of my disapproval was to end the conversation.

I was surprised at how free I felt. As I left the room I felt no resentment. Anger had done its work. Rather than jumping right into a crazy conversation with rage or labored reason—my usual pattern—I spoke and acted differently. Later, my son and I talked about the issue again without blame or lingering resentments. Forgiveness soon followed.

I recall another time, when I was talking on the phone with my mother. At one point in the conversation she said that she did not always feel welcome in my home. This seemed to come right out of the blue. I was tired after teaching all day, and I fell right into the trap. I contradicted her.

My mother, of course, went on to prove her point. She described a visit some five years earlier when, according to her, I had not really welcomed her. I asked her what I had done to cause her discomfort, and she said that she could not recall the details. I remembered the visit well; she had cut the visit short by a week, leaving suddenly and in silence, without any explanation.

In the midst of that phone conversation, I had a flash of anger. "Mother," I said, "we have had this same old conversation my whole life, and the real title of it is 'You don't love me.' I am not having this conversation again." And I said it with conviction and passion.

I could not believe that I said all that. I do not know where the words came from, but I do remember how free I felt. I was able to tell my mother that I regretted her discomfort and that I hoped whatever happened would not happen again. I told her that I loved her and that I did not want her to feel pain in our relationship—and I told her that we would have to find other things to talk about in the future.

My anger at my mother's behavior cleared the air for me. I had stood up and said, "No. No more." I had interrupted the old song-and-dance routine we had been doing for many years. Although I certainly didn't realize it in the moment, forgiveness had begun. I asked my mother to write me a letter stating what she wanted from me as a daughter. She said that she had never really thought about that, but she complied.

My mother wrote of her need for respect and explained that she was too old and too tired to go into all her issues. But that was enough; our relationship improved and our conversations changed. I think she struggled to forgive me for whatever I had done to cause her to feel unwelcome, but we never talked about the issues. We settled into a kind of peaceful coexistence, and at that particular time in our relationship, peaceful coexistence was a welcome improvement.

Logical consequence says, "If you persist in stepping on my foot I will not stand next to you." So often we're inclined to make the offender move; we would rather change the offender than do the work we have to do ourselves. Sooner or later, however, we learn that this is impossible. We cannot change other people. We can change only our own behavior. We can use anger to speak up and change the situation from our side.

Exercise

In this exercise, you will look at how you might change the situation with the offender, from your side. In the previous story about the telephone call with my mother, I interrupted the pattern of arguments so familiar to us and did something very different. I said, "No." My anger led me to say "Enough is enough." I was able to speak clearly about what I would no longer do, what I hoped would happen between us in the future, and how I would act/what I would do to bring this about.

Return to the two sentences about your resentments. (See page 45.) With the information from each of them, complete the following sentences:

(Name of offender), no. I will no longer be a party to or participate in (the offensive behavior/situation). Instead I will (name or describe your specific intentions for change in as much detail as you need).

For further reflection: Reread your intentions. Be sure they are all "I" statements about you and your intentions, and not statements which blame the offender. Your intentions should be positive actions which can set you free from the negative patterns of communication with or about the offender. They should not be dependent on the behavior of the offender.

This exercise will begin to move you to change old habits and point you toward a more positive future. You may return to it as often as you need, until you feel secure, confident, and clear about your intentions and what you truly want for yourself. It may be inappropriate to state your intentions to the offender; it is enough for now that you state them for yourself.

Conclusion

A second roadblock to forgiveness is the double-sided reaction to anger. We have every right to be angry when we have been hurt, but we usually erupt into rage we cannot control, or descend into a resigned acceptance of pain and alienation.

Yet, anger is an energy that can propel us beyond these obstacles. It generates the energy that is needed to sort out the issues of any given situation. It directs us to name our truths and move toward positive changes. Anger is a force that enables us to set boundaries for ourselves and empowers us with renewed self-respect.

Forgiveness often needs a good dose of anger to get it going. Forgiveness as seen here is an invitation to redeem failure, to change your actions that have failed you and the relationship, and to act in different ways that will bring new life.

When you come to grips with your anger, when you befriend it, when you practice using it, you make great progress in the process of forgiveness.

Prayer

Source of Energy and New Life,

You bind up the wounds left from my mindless rages
*   and consecrate me for constructive actions.*
You keep vigil as I stretch to discover my deepest truths,
*   as I tremble to make changes in my life.*

Calm me, gentle me now
*   as I move within to explore shadows and reflections in the*
*   recesses of my mind.*
Still me so I can begin to sense beneath and beyond
*   mere appearances.*
*   Give me the vision to behold the unexpected.*

Be for me the fresh surprise in the old memory,
*   the new horizon just around the bend.*
Source of Light, kindle the spark of my imagination.

6

RECOVERING IMAGINATION

The Enlightenment, which began in the seventeenth century, was a time dedicated to human reason. Scientists told the world that the only reality was that which could be impartially observed.

As a result, people became suspicious of human feelings. Feelings were relegated to the world of women in the home, not to the world of men in the laboratory. Feelings were unstable because they could not be examined and measured under the microscope.

Naturally, human imagination also came under suspicion because it could not be controlled and scientifically measured. The imagination was fine for children, but it did not belong in the world of thoughts and reason. Thus science took the place of faith, and the human person was divided into compartments.

It has taken hundreds of years to rediscover our wholeness, to appreciate, celebrate, and nurture the whole man and the whole woman as people who use reason, express feelings, and have lively imaginations. We are beginning to retrieve and honor the role of imagination in our lives. We are relearning the importance of feelings and reclaiming the importance of the imagination. We now know that the imagination is one of our most critical resources.

IMAGINATION AND FAITH

Our imagination is a powerful entity. It can cause the hair on the back of our neck to stand up, the spirit to soar, the face to blush. Imagination is the power that holds our beliefs together; we believe with our imagination. The imagination is the wellspring of faith and hope. Our biggest and best dreams for ourselves and others rise from the imagination.

When we have been hurt, our imagination is wounded. As a result, alienation and belief in bad news replace belief in good news. For example, when we have been injured by another, we have a feeling response that can become frozen into resentment. We have an anger response that can become frozen into negative reactions of rage or passivity.

We also have an interpretation response. As we continue to see the offender and ourselves in a less positive light, we become frozen in negative attitudes, perceptions, biases, and beliefs. In some cases we hold on to these as if the offense happened yesterday; in some cases, we actually enjoy holding on to the pain of these experiences. As a result, the imagination becomes paralyzed. Attending to the wounded imagination is the third path through forgiveness.

In previous chapters, we worked with the resentments we cling to and the anger we ignore, both impediments to forgiveness. We now look at interpretations that we have consciously or unconsciously come to believe.

EXERCISE

To experience how your imagination works, close your eyes, picture your bedroom, and count the pieces of furniture in it. This is putting your imagination to work. You used your imagination in the final exercise in chapter 5 when you imagined what you might do and say to the offender. (See page 56.) When you described feelings in chapter 4, you used images, like "a rug was pulled out from under me." That, too, was a use of your imagination. (See page 44.)

This exercise relies even more directly on your imagination. It will be easier for some but possible for all. You are going to use images as windows through which to look at the offender and yourself. The images will be various colors.

I share with you my own experience of this exercise. When I picture my mother angry and silent, I see her as the color black because she seems so dark and foreboding. She seems mysterious to me. I see myself as the color beige because beige is a weak, nondescriptive color; it blends into the surroundings.

When I see my mother pushing me to succeed, I see her as the color red because she expended so much passion in what I thought was nagging. For me red is the color of fury. I see myself as the color purple. Purple reminds me of sadness and mourning. Our relationship sometimes made me sad. Purple is a mixture of red and blue. Maybe I choose purple because I know at some deep level that I have some of my mother in me.

Write these sentences and fill in the blanks. (Note: This exercise can also be done using various animals or the seasons of the year instead of colors.)

When I see (the offender) as (the offending action) I see him (or her) as the color _____ because _____.
I see myself as the color _____ because

_____.

For further reflection: Why did you choose the colors you did? These choices point to and force you to verbalize deeper positive and negative beliefs about the offender and yourself, beliefs and assumptions that often are hidden from consciousness. Do your images of color disclose new insights? Do you experience any shocks of recognition?

IMAGINATION AND PERCEPTION

Is the glass of water half-full or half-empty? The answer depends entirely on how you see it. "How you see it" is called "perception."

There is the story about the blind men and the elephant. Each man named and described the animal according to his experience of touching only one part of the elephant's body. The man who held the trunk "perceived" the elephant to be a large snake; the man who held the leg "perceived" the elephant to be a sturdy tree. In the same way, we "perceive" life—depending on what our experience is.

Our experiences generate our expectations. For example, if we are criticized by the office manager, we come to expect criticism on the job. If we are treated with respect by a coworker we come to expect a pleasant en-

counter whenever we meet. Our daily experiences form our almost uncon-
scious expectations of others.

Our experiences also generate our perceptions. We experience and expect criticism from the office manager and begin to perceive and label
that person as hostile and overcritical. We experience and expect a pleasant encounter with the coworker, and perceive that person to be good-
natured. Repeated encounters with these two people will only serve to
confirm and deepen our perceptions.

Our perceptions are the source of our likes, dislikes, and feelings; they
dictate our responses and actions. We "can't stand" and therefore avoid
the office manager; we feel comfortable around and therefore seek out the
coworker.

This is typical human behavior. The problem occurs when we get stuck
in negative perceptions of others, when we cannot or will not take another
look or give the person another chance. We have grown to believe that this
is the way they always were and always will be. We have developed what
our popular culture calls an "attitude."

Perceptions can last a lifetime. It may be difficult for an older sibling,
for example, to see a younger sibling as an adult and not just "my little
brother, the goof-off." Old attitudes and viewpoints die hard because they
often remain unchallenged and unexamined.

I have a friend whose older brother was very unpleasant to her for as
long as she could remember. When the brother had a stroke and recovered,
he was completely different; he seemed to forget that he ever disliked his
sister. As a result, his sister was forced to look at her brother differently.
Today the two are very close.

We interpret life experiences, and we form expectations and perceptions, attitudes and assumptions. All of this activity is the work of the
imagination. It is likewise the work of the imagination to reinterpret and
reform repeated assumptions and expectations.

IMAGINATION AND MEMORY

I am fascinated with family photograph albums. The photos that
find their way into albums are chosen for how they depict the people and
their relationships to one another. These carefully crafted albums are ar-
ranged to tell the family story in a particular way. They are interpreted
history.

Yet, one photograph album does not tell the whole story. "There is always more than meets the eye," says an old adage. Each person in the family will tell a family story differently. Brothers and sisters recall their parents in such diverse ways that we may wonder if they all grew up in the same family.

Each member of a family has his or her own experience and no one member has the whole picture. The problem is that most of us believe we do have the whole picture. We think that our memories are objective newsreels, when in fact they are selected interpretations.

Our memories often need correction. Was my mother angry and silent all the time? My brother remembers her laughing at our father's jokes. She encouraged his goofy humor. I had forgotten about those wonderful, silly jokes and how my mother loved them. Now I remember.

Memory is always faulty because it is always incomplete. Did my parents argue a lot? My cousin reminds me of how much they enjoyed going out for dinner together and taking long rides on Sunday afternoons. I did not remember that part of my family history.

Family members need to come together and compare memories and mental snapshots if they want to see and understand how parents and children interacted on a larger scale. Such "reality checks" help enlarge and critique individual interpretations. Forgiveness demands that we take another look so that the imagination can reframe our narrow interpretations. Sometimes forgiveness demands that we check out our impressions with others.

About ten years ago I was packing to return home after a visit to Louisiana. At the last minute my mother gave me an envelope containing a few old photographs. Weeks later, when I sat down and looked through them, I found pictures of my parents before I was born. There were several of my mother as a little girl. I had never seen a picture of her as a child.

The pictures show my mother feeding chickens, holding a rabbit, lying on her stomach in a field with her chin propped up in her hands, always smiling at the unseen photographer. Her hair is the typical straight, bob cut and bangs of that era. She was a cute little girl.

I began to think about her childhood and some of the things she had told me over the years. Her mother died when she was two years old, and she was raised by her father and an older sister. Her chore was to milk the cows every morning before school. She graduated first in her class and wanted to go to college, but there was no money for tuition.

My parents were married when my mother was nineteen. She worked as a secretary and could type a perfect one hundred twenty-five words a minute. She sewed beautifully. She always wanted to have children.

One of the photographs of my parents sits on my desk. It was taken during the Depression, when they were quite young. The picture shows my parents sitting on a brick wall, my mother leaning against my father, smiling. I know they had dreams for their future and very little money. I know that many of their dreams were lost over the years.

Thinking about the past and the people who lived there can enlarge the horizon of memory. I can begin to see much more than my own memory allowed. Some things were probably better than I imagined and others were more negative than I remembered. Forgiveness expands our horizons and invites us to retrieve the positive and work through the negative.

EXERCISE

Recall some of the events and circumstances that you know occurred in the life of the offender. Take some time and think about this and make a list. Write facts not opinions. Think of these facts as stepping stones in the offender's life. Make a list of at least ten events and circumstances.

For further reflection: What insights do you discover as you begin to see this person in a broader context? Is there any shift in your perceptions? Is there any softening of the negatives? Is there any unexpected positive discovery?

IMAGINATION AND FORGIVENESS

When we begin to ponder the pieces of another's life story we begin to see a bigger picture. There is more to the offender's life than the negative piece we own, no matter how much we want to believe otherwise. Part of the forgiveness process is forcing ourselves to look at this. Forgiveness includes the decision to refocus.

In *Learning To Forgive* (Abingdon Press, 1986), author Doris Donnelly calls this process "enlarging the context." When we see more pieces to the picture, we begin to see the offender as more than the occasion of our suffering. Native Americans speak of walking a mile in another's moccasins; this is the experience we're looking for. We begin to understand the world in which the other lives and the context that shaped her or him. The issues may remain the same, but our perspective on them changes.

Embracing parts of my mother's history affected me. I began to understand some of her behaviors. For example, since her mother died when she was only two years old, she had no role model for the task of mothering. I can barely imagine what it must have been like not to have a mother.

Of course, I still do not approve of some of my mother's actions toward me, but she did the best she could with the knowledge and experience she had. I think I did the best I could, too, although I wanted more. Now I am beginning to believe that what I received from my mother was enough. She shaped me into the person I am today, and I know she was very proud to have me as her daughter.

Seeing the offender in a broader context creates space to revise interpretations and soften expectations. Seeing a bigger picture makes room for a bigger story. When our limited picture of the offender is altered, so is the story we tell.

When I was six years old, all my girlfriends had WAC uniforms purchased from the local dry goods store. I wanted one in the worst way, so my mother made a copy of the uniform for me from one of my father's worn-out suits. Although the other mothers admired my mother's sewing, I was embarrassed. I never let on.

Everyone, including my mother, said that my uniform looked just like the "real thing," that I looked just like the other girls. I never knew if this was true or not, but I secretly wished I had the "real thing." As the years passed I rarely thought about this event, but when I did, I dismissed it as another example of how my mother always got her way.

I tell the story differently now. For me this is the story about a woman who was both caring and proud, about my mother who truly wanted to give me what I wanted. The time was World War II. My father worked at an oil refinery and my mother had lost her job. They had little money. This is a story about an ingenious solution to a child's desires. It really is a love story.

Notice how I have not changed the story. I simply see it through a wider lens. This is the work of the imagination. Remembering the story as one of embarrassment and ego was not wrong. Those pieces are true. But remembering the story only in that way robs it of its good news, of its power to reveal deeper truths.

Our imagination invites us to return to the "bad news" stories about the offender and to take another look. The story of the WAC uniform has power for me because it speaks to me of how much my parents loved me and to what lengths those two struggling people would go to care for me, even when I could not see it. Today it is a story about my parents that I am proud to tell.

Exercise

Give yourself at least fifteen minutes with no interruptions to write this reflection. You may want to turn off the phone and set a timer.

Reread what you wrote in the list of stepping stones in the life of the offender. (See page 64.) Let that person's life events be present to you.

Now write a letter to yourself from the offender. Say all the things you always wanted her or him to say to you. Do not hold back on this. Be lavish. This is a gift to yourself. Begin with "Dear, <u>(your name)</u>," and write for as long as you want, but no less than fifteen minutes. Sign the letter "From <u>(the offender's name)</u>," and date it.

For further reflection: How did you feel writing this letter? Read the letter aloud. How do you feel hearing these words?

We deserve to hear these words because in the quiet of our hearts we know they are true. Different circumstances in the life of the offender might have allowed the offender to write them personally. Because he or she could not offer you these words in person does not mean they are not true.

You can use this exercise often and with other offenders who have harmed you. Writing the letter can help you realize that it is not too late to replace bad news with more positive memories—and to forgive. It will help you receive the love and respect you deserve.

Conclusion

We have seen that the third roadblock to forgiveness resides in the imagination. When we hold onto the belief that our perception of the offender and the offense is the whole picture, we fail to believe in or understand the process of forgiveness.

If we stick to a negative interpretation of an old offense, we will experience resentment whenever we think about it or about the offender. We will never be able to grieve and let go; we will seesaw between rage and resignation; we will never allow anger to surface and put us back on the journey of forgiveness.

If we insist on telling and retelling our bad news stories of the past, we simply recycle the bad news and pass it on to the next generation. We pollute the emotional environment; we remain stuck in lifeless memories instead of looking for a more positive side of things long past.

When you enlarge your perceptions you at least allow for the possibility of healing. You give yourself the opportunity to turn from the negative aspects of your past, to get rid of the excess baggage, and to face the journey into the future with hope.

PRAYER

Holy One, Beyond All the Names I Give You,

I believe you are the horizon which I seek
and the path which leads me there.
I believe you are the beginning and the end of my journey,
and I praise and thank you for your invitation to come to you.

Send your spirit of forgiveness and prepare my heart
to discover and embrace your gift of reconciliation.
Make of me a forgiving presence to your creation,
to see as you see, love as you love.

Mentor me always, Forgiving One,
in the art of forgiveness.
Forever and ever.

FINAL THOUGHTS

A WELCOME

At the beginning, you were offered an invitation to make a journey. You accepted. You gave your presence. You fully participated. You displayed courage. You listened well to the prophet and the evangelist: "Return to me with your whole heart. Repent and believe the gospel." Welcome to this space.

The good news here is the realization that forgiveness is not confined to the pulpit and to the pages of romance novels. Forgiveness is not something you only hear or read about. It is there—here—for you in your everyday living.

At the beginning of this experience you read about the pope's visit to Rome's Rebibbia Prison in the winter of 1984. You considered the lessons that story of forgiveness offers today. You then began your own exploration of forgiveness and learned that it is quite different from what you probably had been led to believe. Forgiveness is not approval, the immediate restoration of trust, or the interruption of logical consequences.

These insights were intended to free you from old psychological baggage as you explored a new path through the pain of alienation. The journey of forgiveness invited you to embrace your broken heart, confront your useless reactions, and refocus your narrow, negative interpretations. You worked with resentments, anger, and negative images in order to grieve painful losses, speak your truth, and enlarge your perceptions of reality.

A FINAL EXERCISE

Here is a final set of "writing lines." Choose the sentence that suits you best right now, and fill in the blanks. Remember, you can return to this reflection in the future.

_____, I forgive you for _____.
_____, I am trying to forgive you for _____.
_____, someday I hope to forgive you for _____.
_____, at this time the pain is still too fresh for me to forgive you for _____.

For further reflection: Which sentence did you choose? Which do you hope to choose next year at this time? What can you add to the list of definitions of forgiveness? What do you want to do now that you understand more about forgiveness? Are you ready to consider forgiving the people you love to hate? How will you celebrate your journey to this moment?

SEIZED BY GRACE

Forgiveness is your job. It is what you must do. Reconciliation is God's job. You do not make reconciliation happen. You make forgiveness happen; God takes care of the rest.

You need not be afraid. Reconciliation will never lead you backward to the former status quo. It steals upon you gently and leads you to a new place. It is a place of peace, freedom, wisdom, and trust. It is a place where your capacity for joy and sorrow is deepened. It is God's gift waiting to be found.

Reconciliation is not to be confused with resignation. You do not resign yourself to the situations in your life with a long sigh of abdication to the cruel twists of fate. You discover something quite different.

One summer day I was walking down a city street to a friend's apartment. In spite of the beautiful sunshine, I was in a bad mood, and I cannot remember why. As I bought a bouquet of flowers from a corner vendor to cheer myself, I spied a street woman familiar to everyone in the neighborhood: "Crazy Annie" we called her. She was harmless, but I wanted to avoid her so I pretended not to see her. As we passed each other I felt her hand on my shoulder. I was caught—and my mood worsened.

I was embarrassed to be seen with Crazy Annie; she smelled and talked loudly. While she asked me where I was going, who my friend was, and a litany of other questions, I was rude and tried to brush her off. She reached out and touched the flowers and said they were beautiful—and then she touched my cheek and said that I was beautiful too.

I had to smile and shake my head, at both Annie's goodness and my lack of charity. Instantly I had a mental image of Jesus turning to the crowd and saying, "O you scribes and pharisees, which of these two women do you think will enter the kingdom of heaven first?"

In a flash, Annie called me out of my self-imposed alienation, and I was reconciled to the goodness of life through her. I was both repentant and grateful. I embraced Annie and gave her the flowers.

I call this story "Seized by Grace." This is what happened in the lives of those we read about earlier. In the midst of mourning the death of her daughter, Betty was led to a deeper relationship with God. She realized that she was being led through her grief toward a new way of being in life. She tells about a time when she was sitting quietly in her house and had the overwhelming sense that her daughter was near and at peace. This brought Betty a deep sense of serenity. Several years later, when Betty and I were at the bedside of a dying friend, she leaned down and whispered, "When you see Suzanne tell her that her mother is all right too."

Carol was led to trust her potential and to start a new life. From within the midst of her pain and alienation, she discovered the capacity for new life hidden. Her support group of wonderful friends helped her move on. Her children are grown now, and she is a grandmother.

The man on the jury emerged from the ordeal of his son's murder believing again in people and in the process of life. His spirit remains so much with me today that I actually found myself looking around for him when I recently was called back for potential jury duty. I let my mind travel back to that time nearly ten years ago, and I silently thanked that gentle man for his part in my understanding of forgiveness.

The journey of forgiveness takes patience and time, and often demands repeating. Active waiting, too, is a part of that journey. We watch; we listen. We lean toward the future, and we bow in prayer. We stand in hope. And one day we discover God's gracious presence rising from within.

PRAYER

Gracious God,

You call me to yourself,
to flood me and fill me with your reconciling presence.
You call me near to proclaim to me who you are,
and to reveal to me who I am in your eyes.
I stand ready to receive your words and your revelation.
Speak to me your cherished words of healing, O God.

"Do you know who you are?
I have probed you and I know you.
I know when you sit and when you stand.
I understand your thoughts from far away
and know every detail of your journey.

"If you go to the heavens I am there.
If you sink to the nether world I am present with you there.
If you take the winds of dawn and settle at the farthest
limits of the sea even
there my hand shall guide you.
I am behind you and before you.

"Do you know who you are?
I called you before you were born,
from your mother's womb I pronounced your name.
Can a mother forget her baby at her breast,
or fail to cherish the child of her womb?
Yet even if she forgets, I will never forget you.

"Do you know who you are?
You are fearfully and wonderfully made.
I formed your innermost being and knitted you in secret.

I have brushed away all your offenses like a cloud,
  your sins like a mist.

"I place gladness in your heart and guide you in the
  right paths of action.
I enlighten your sight and put a new song on your lips,
  a song of good news.
Look, upon the palms of my hands
  I have written your name.
I call you by name. You are my delight.
  You are my beloved.

"Do you know?"

Bibliography

Augsburger, David W. *Caring Enough to Forgive*. Ventura, Calif.: Regal Books, 1981.

Brady, Loretta. *Beginning Your Enneagram Journey*. Chicago: Thomas More Press, 1994.

Donnelly, Doris. *Learning To Forgive*. Nashville: Abingdon Press, 1986.

Donovan, Vincent J. *Christianity Rediscovered*. Maryknoll, N.Y.: Orbis Books, 1982.

Frankl, Viktor E. *Man's Search for Meaning*. New York: New American Library, 1969.

Halpern, Howard M. *Cutting Loose*. New York: Simon and Schuster, 1990.

Jenco, Lawrence M., OSB. *Bound to Forgive: The Pilgrimage to Reconciliation of a Beruit Hostage*. Notre Dame: Ave Maria Press, 1995.

Killen, Patricia O'Connell and John DeBeer. *The Art of Theological Reflection*. New York: Crossroad, 1994.

Lewis, C. S. *A Grief Observed*. New York: The Seabury Press, 1961.

Luebering, Carol. *The Forgiving Family: First Steps to Reconciliation*. Cincinnati: St. Anthony Messenger Press, 1983.

Morrow, Lance, reported by Barry Kalb and Wilton Wynn (Rome). "I Spoke...As a Brother." *Time* (January 9, 1984): pp. 27-33.

Powell, John. *Happiness Is an Inside Job*. Allen, Tex.: Tabor Publishing, 1989.

————. *Solving the Riddle of Self: The Search for Self-Discovery*. Allen, Tex.: Tabor Publishing, 1995.

Schreiter, Robert J., ed. *Reconciliation: Mission and Ministry in a Changing Social Order*. Maryknoll, N.Y.: Orbis Books, 1992.

Smedes, Lewis B. *Forgive and Forget: Healing the Hurts We Don't Deserve*. San Francisco: Harper & Row, 1991.

Viorst, Judith. *Necessary Losses*. New York: Fawcett, 1987.

Whitehead, James D. and Evelyn E. *Shadows of the Heart: A Spirituality of the Negative Emotions*. New York: Crossroad, 1994.

ABOUT THE AUTHOR

Judy Logue is a popular speaker and workshop presenter. She designed and facilitates "The Martha Retreat" for women who are busy about many things. Logue is the director of her parish RCIA, and Director of Continuing Lay Formation for the Catholic Theological Union in Chicago.

More spiritual guidebooks from Liguori...

DAILY STRENGTH
One Year of Experiencing the Psalms
Victor M. Parachin
"Provides comfort and guidance in daily doses from one of the all-time greatest sources of spiritual strength." (*Christian Retailing,* March 1, 1995) **$12.95**

THE HEALING POWER OF PRAYER
Bridget Mary Meehan
Rooted in Christian tradition and Scripture, this book examines approaches to inner healing that will lead you to experience the healing love of God in your life. Healing prayer is a life-changing force that will give you new freedom while you learn to forgive, become more aware of your own limitations, and develop a greater sensitivity to the needs of others. **$9.95**

HOW TO FORGIVE YOURSELF AND OTHERS
(REVISED AND EXPANDED)
Steps to Reconciliation
Rev. Eamon Tobin
An updated guide to forgiveness. All the helpful material of the original, plus new guidelines to forgiving a deceased person, new sections on forgiving God and the Church, and an expanded section on forgiveness of self. **$3.95**

Order from your local bookstore or write to:
Liguori Publications
Box 060, Liguori, MO 63057-9999
Please add 15% of your total to your order ($3.50 minimum, $15 maximum) for shipping and handling. For faster service on orders over $20 call toll-free 1-800-325-9521, Dept. 060. Please have your credit card ready.